I Know HE Cares For me

by Jerry Petty

Battling with Muscular Dystrophy and Trusting God

Chosen Word Publishing
Charlotte, North Carolina

Scriptures taken from King James Version

ISBN 09754779-7-8
$12.95

Published by Chosen Word Publishing, Charlotte, N.C.
www.chosenwordpublishing.com

You may contact Jerry Petty at:
jerry@chosenwordpublishing.com

A very special thanks to Josh Mangum for the beautiful cover design.

DEDICATION

I dedicate this book to my mother, Myra Davis and my loving family. A special Thank You to all of you for the smallest to the greatest things you've done for me.

A special thanks to MDA for all of the help you've given me over the years.

A NOTE FROM THE PUBLISHER

I would like to thank Jerry Perry for giving Chosen Word Publishing the honor of publishing his book, *I Know HE Cares For Me*. I spent many hours reading and reviewing his manuscript. This book impacted my life and I could not put it down until I was finished.

Jerry Petty is a perfect picture of love and respect. Reading this book gave me a totally different perspective about people with disabilities. He is truly a warrior that refuses to bow down to the odds that are stacked against him.

I continued to hear the silent screams of a young man that loves God and has strong determination in reaching his goals.

His unique perspective on love and life should be shared throughout the world. I believe this book will change and touch the lives of people with and without disabilities. It will also assist in removing societal barriers that face people with disabilities. Although this book has been edited, we made the decision to keep it as close to Jerry's voice as possible. His words are heartfelt and honest. Jerry has difficulty with his speech but writing is the only avenue he has to completely express himself. We will miss the point if we concentrate on how he says it, opposed to the point he is attempting to convey.

May God Bless You Jerry, as you emerge into your destiny.

Jeannette T. Gregory, Publisher
Chosen Word Publishing, Inc.

FOREWORD

It gives me great pleasure to write the Foreword for *I Know He Cares for Me*. Jerry has talked about this book for so many years and finally it has come to fruition! In spite of his struggle with completing this book due to the limited use of his arms, hands and continued computer problems, He made it!

I have known Jerry and Mother Myra for many years. We met at MDA Summer Camp about 16 years ago and over the years Jerry has come to know my family also. With all of his day to day struggles he always thinks of others first. There is not a time that we meet and Jerry doesn't ask how my Mom, Dad and my daughter are doing.

Fate has connected our paths on many occasions. I specifically remember about 10 years ago when I was driving through Charlotte with a friend. Suddenly, I made an unexpected detour to drive past a friend's house. That friend was Jerry Petty. I had not driven by his house for at least a year or two but on this cold day as I approached his house I could see his wheelchair turned sideways and Jerry lying on the ground. He calmly asked if I could find someone to help me get him and his wheelchair back upright. I ran to a neighbor and he kindly came to assist.

Jerry quietly and shyly requested a big favor from me. Of course I responded, "Sure, anything." He said, "Please do not tell my mother about this because I don't want to worry her in the future." He explained that his mother had to work while he stayed at home and he just didn't want to worry her. I gave Jerry my promise but the funny thing is the next time I saw Jerry and his mom, Myra said "Jerry told me what happened". That didn't surprise me one bit. Jerry and his Mother are two of the finest people in this world, best friends to each other and anyone they meet.

Once you begin to read this book it will be impossible to put it down. This book gives you a brief summary of a young man with a progressive disease that eventually disables his body but seems to strengthen his heart, mind and soul.

The main point that this book conveys to its readers is: Treat people with disabilities with the same level of respect and consideration that you have for others. This book comes from the heart of a man that has endured many obstacles and has overcome more than most of us could ever imagine.

Each page is filled with love, forgiveness, appreciation, faith, and care for your fellow man and woman.

As Jerry says, "Treat others with respect, never stare at a person without saying hello, teach your children to speak to those with disabilities and ask questions." They may be lucky enough to meet someone as wonderful as Jerry, just as I did 16 years ago!

Todd Dewey

ABOUT THE AUTHOR

My name is Jerry Lamont Petty and I was born on August 21, 1976 in Charlotte, North Carolina. My mother's name is Myra Petty and my father's name is Jerry Lewis Petty. My stepbrother's are Ryan Petty, 15 years old and Clark Petty, 13.

I graduated from East Mecklenburg High School in Charlotte, N.C. on June 3, 1994. I am now 28 years old and I haven't walked since the age of 12 because I was born with Muscular Dystrophy.

I have always been considered as "the lucky one to be alive" because I've lost so many of my friends to this disease.

My disability requires the use of a wheelchair because I lost a lot of strength in my arms and legs. My mother is always there to help me and I am so blessed to have a mother like her.

It seems as if my hands and shoulders get weaker and weaker as the days get longer. The degeneration of the skeletal or voluntary muscles which control movement, at a slow process, my muscles give out and I'm unable to do anything for myself.

I really miss walking and being able to move around by myself. Even though I wasn't able to run fast and keep up with the other kids, I still miss being able to walk. Being young and having to deal with the stress from my disability and the cruelness from the children at school brought on a lot of added and unnecessary stress for me.

CONTENTS

CONTENTS

MY MOTHER

My mother has taken care of me my entire life. She has done so many wonderful things for me. I think accepting me as her son, just the way I am is all I ever needed from her.

She is a very strong hearted woman and I wouldn't be here if it weren't for her and God. My mother is a blessing from God and she is also my friend.

My advice to everyone who has a mother, whether you are healthy or sick, remember that it is so important to have her in your life. Be grateful of her, respect her and treat her like the Queen that she is.

My mother and I have come a long way through many struggles, stress and pressure, but we made it by the grace of God. My mother always says to me, "God is always listening to us and He will get us through the drama in our lives."

LEARNING TO FORGIVE

My father and I really don't have anything in common. Maybe it's because he was never around for me and my mom. The majority of the time I was filled with disappointment because I didn't have my father in my life. Gradually, the anger and rage continued to build because he wasn't there to be the father when I needed him the most.

I think it would have made me feel better if he had said, "I'll come by to visit sometimes." Unfortunately, there were no phone calls and several months would go by without my seeing him.

I could not understand why my father could not accept me as his son or make any efforts to learn anything about me. I'm sure that he had no idea what my mom and I were going through.

The main question that I needed an answer for is, "Why couldn't he accept me as his oldest son?"
No matter what, I still love my dad because I'm still apart of him.

I KNOW HE CARES FOR ME

Because my heavenly Father cares for me, no matter who I am or what my disabilities are, HE CARES.

I had to forgive my father for everything I thought he did not do or for some things he did that I did not understand. My heart and soul will not allow me to hate him and because of this, “I am free.” It is my prayer that he be the father that he needs to be to his other sons.

God wants us to love and not hate. Love releases all of the anger built up inside of you.

43 "You have heard that it was said, 'You shall love your neighbor and hate your enemy.' 44 *But I say to you, love your enemies, bless those who curse you, do good to those who hate you, and pray for those who spitefully use you and persecute you, 45 that you may be sons of your Father in heaven; for He makes His sun rise on the evil and on the good, and sends rain on the just and on the unjust. 46 For if you love those who love you, what reward have you? Matthew 5:43-46*

My heart is healing from all of the love that my family gives to me. Most of all, the love that God gives me is the healer, because HE CARES.

GOOD TIMES

I've had some really good times in my life and the memories will last forever. I remember my first airplane ride when I flew to Dallas, Texas and San Diego, California for summer camp for three days. I met a lot of wonderful people who later became my dear friends.

I was very nervous about meeting new people because I was very shy. Instead, I found out that they were very receptive of me.

I had a great time on the beach and I went on a big boat. "Can you imagine Jerry Petty on a boat?" We visited Sea World and it was amazing. There was plenty of good food to eat and I enjoyed it . . . but. . .I still missed my mother. This was the first time in my life that I had been so many miles away from her. I was 2,000 miles from home and it took a lot of courage to get on that big plane without my mom.

I was attending a summer camp with MDA and I enjoyed those 3 days in San Diego, California but it was good to land in Charlotte, N.C.

That trip in 1993 was a good experience and one of the best times I've had in my entire life.

MEETING NEW FRIENDS

It was very difficult for me to meet new friends and communicate effectively with them. Even though I was very shy, I had a crush on a girl in Junior High. I see her in my dreams all of the time. She was special to me and she didn't even know it. I thought she was the most beautiful girl in the world but I never told her how I felt about her. I can't help but wonder how she felt about being involved with someone who is disabled. I pray that she is in good health and wish her much success in life.

I had another crush on a girl that I will not reveal her name. She was a pretty girl back in Junior High and I met her in P.E. class. We talked briefly but I didn't know what to talk about or how to ask her for her number. I would panic every time I saw her.

I still have that fear of meeting a nice lady friend and I wonder why people can't see around the wheelchair. I feel as though I know how to treat a lady and love her the way she deserves to be loved. I guess I blew my chance with her. She would always speak to me in class because she was a wonderful person. I would like the opportunity to tell her that she will always have a place in my heart. I don't have a problem talking to ladies now. Without revealing her identity, I would like to say to her, "You were a truly beautiful lady, thank you for speaking. God bless you."

CRAZY LOVE

Finally, I met my true love, the only girl I ever asked to marry me. She attended West Mecklenburg too. We became very close after we graduated and became best friends. We have been friends for 13 years.
No matter what was going on, she kept a big smile on her face. I just knew she was the one and only love for me.

Our relationship was special and we were very close. We were able to talk about our feelings and goals for the future and we will forever have that special bond between us.

She taught me so many things such as, the meaning of friendship and what real love is. She helped me through the rough times in my life and I cared deeply for her and wanted to keep her safe.

I wanted to be a good man for her but sadly, our relationship ended in 1997 and it was not easy to let her go but we will remain close friends forever.

In my heart, she will always be my girl and I wish that we could have married and had a family together. That would've been a wonderful thing to happen to us.

One of the things that we had in common was, her father wasn't around and she went through some rough times. I tried to encourage her to move on with her life, be happy and keep her faith strong. I still love her dearly. Maybe someday we will get back together.
As of now, I try to stay focused and concentrate on my life and move on.

ROLE MODEL

My step dad was a good role model for me and he was always there for my mother. We are blessed to still have him in our lives. I wouldn't trade him for anything in the world because he is a great guy.

He's always telling funny jokes, even though none of them really made any sense. My step dad has a unique way of making you feel comfortable and welcome. He is a great cook that makes sure that every one has enough to eat. He has 3 daughters who are wonderful sisters to me. My mom and step dad's marriage ended 3 years ago but they still remain close friends.

I would like to say thank you to my step dad for being a positive role model for me.

FOR WHEN I AM WEAK, THEN I AM STRONG

When I was growing up, I felt like I was disconnected from this world. I was constantly picked on by kids at school who would turn on me for no reason at all. It was difficult to make friends because my way of communicating was a little different from theirs.

My question then and still is, "Why do people tend to lose their compassion, love and consideration for others?" How can something so precious be lost? Somehow, I wish people could walk in my shoes, feel my pain and see what I go through on a daily basis. Even as I write this book I continue to ask the question, "Why me? I didn't do anything wrong or bad."

I don't like living with this horrible disease but I realized that God made me special so that I could teach people around me what love and faith are really all about.
I used to cry to myself everyday as I blamed the world for my fears.

Many times I gave up on life and felt sorry for myself. My faith in God was failing as I stopped trusting Him in the low periods in my life.

When I concentrated on the hurt of not having a father around to talk to about the male aspects on life, my mind would just begin to go crazy.

When I was younger, I found myself not wanting to be around people because they could walk. I know that I will never walk again and this disease has ruined my life. But yet, at the same time, it has been a blessing to me.

I also felt distance from my family because I didn't want them to feel sorry for me because I was disabled and in a wheelchair. I discovered that what makes you weak, will also make you stronger in life. You just have to keep the faith and don't ever give up.

Therefore I take pleasure in infirmities, in reproaches, in necessities, in persecutions, in distresses for Christ's sake: for when I am weak, then am I strong. ***2 Corinthians 12:10***

WHAT IS HANDICAPPED?

Merriam Webster dictionary defines handicapped as: sometimes offensive: having a physical or mental disability; also: to put at a disadvantage.

I don't care for the word *handicap* because people seem to use this word in the wrong way. "Why do people make fun of disabled people? Do they realize that we have feelings too?"

Do you have any idea what it's like to go through life not being able to do what you would like to do? I like to challenge you, the next time you see someone that doesn't look like you and maybe they are disabled, try speaking to them. You will be surprised at the response.

Being disabled has changed my outlook on life, people and faith. I've learned to deal with what life has to offer and accept it for what it really is. I love living and seeing how beautiful my surroundings are.

I love sitting outdoors and writing my stories that gives me peace of mind. I choose to live, and that means to maintain my happiness and what matters most to me while I'm still alive.

We all have some type of handicap. The fact that you can see, hear, talk, walk and your outer appearance looks normal doesn't mean that you have it all together. Sometimes people become so wrapped up in their own world until they feel they are perfect in the sight of God and that is all that matters.

Sometimes people choose not to notice their own weaknesses and fail to get help when it is needed.

Even though I am free in my mind, body and spirit, I appear disabled to them and I am treated as if I don't count. This only makes me strive harder to make a difference in this world.

FAITH

My time at Carolinas Medical Center was a wake up call. I saw Jesus when I was dying in the hospital in 1993. My hospital stay lasted for 1 month and I was very sick and very weak. My body was so tired of living and I was ready to die.

My mother stood by me the entire time as she said, "Son, don't you give up, fight it, fight it, okay, you hang in there Jerry, you are not going to leave me yet son, I love you from my heart."

I could hear my mother's voice when I was dying in the hospital. My grandparents, J.D. and grandma Sarah came to see me, they ministered to me when I was so weak, and they have been the best grandparents to me. I asked them to pray for me, I told them I didn't have much time left on this earth and I could feel it in my heart.

My heart started beating slower and feeling tired, I asked God to give me my spirit back and take all of my weaknesses away.

God had given me my spirit back and I promised myself that I wouldn't go down like that. I don't think about life anymore. With the help of God, I put my life back on track and once again dream of being a famous movie star or screenwriter someday.

I finished school and I'm so happy to be alive and to write this book. I am not going to die and I know that I can finish this manuscript. The vision of Jesus helped me out a lot because the doctors had given up on me and they could do nothing else to help me. It was left up to me to get well and I started to eat again.

The doctors approved my release from the hospital. God had given me my spirit back and I had energy to move around again. My mom was so happy for me.

THE STRUGGLE

I remember when my mother and I were living with my Aunt Theresa and my cousin Maurice. It was so much fun for me because my cousin and I were like brothers. It was cool having someone to talk to and play with me. My cousins, Patrick, Crystal, Maurice and I would get together at our grandparents house on Saturdays and have such a good time listening to music and just having fun.

Those times in my life were also hard for me to deal with because I was unable to move around like my cousins and I couldn't keep up with them. My legs would get tired from standing and I was always falling down.

My cousins would help me get up because they understood my condition and they were willing to help me back to my feet. They realized that I could not do everything that they did and no matter what I went through, they still accepted me as their cousin.

My mother had to have our house reconstructed and made accessible to meet my needs. The bathroom had to be set up for my convenience. Even after the reconstruction, my power wheelchair was still too wide to move freely through the house without getting stuck.

This was corrected by knocking out walls to widen the hallways. My mom has made a lot of sacrifices for me and she means the world to me. She has always kept a roof over my head and made sure that I have everything that I need.

There were times when she would have to lift me in and out of the car whenever we went out. I'm sure that must have been hard for her especially when I started to gain so much weight. She bought a van to accommodate me and had to spend more money to get a lift added on. It is very expensive for disabled people to maintain a normal lifestyle. I can say that my mom has done everything to make sure that I am happy and well taken care of.

LEARNING TO LIVE

My best friend lives in Connecticut. I met her in high school and we kept in touch over the years. It's been almost a year since we last spoke. She has been a great influence in my life and she is a hard worker.

She was in my homeroom class and I started to care for her as we wrote letters to each other. It was the same feelings I felt for my first true love. I will never forget all the good times we had together.

I love and respect women for more than just good looks and their bodies. I am happy with a woman who can just accept me for who I am.

It is my belief that most men can't be happy with just one woman; they fail to realize that they could be missing out on someone special when they don't take the time to really get to know her.

Sometimes I feel that people need to be reborn and start their lives over. They need to learn how to treat people with disabilities and show them the same respect as they give people who are healthy and appear to be normal.

I don't hear enough talk about love and bringing people together. I hear a lot about people killing each other and it really shouldn't be that way.

Sometimes the world seems so sad and cold. I realize that nobody is perfect but we need to work together and believe in each other, start rebuilding and educating our children.

Our children need to be educated at home as well as in the classroom. I feel it is the parents' responsibility to teach their children the true meaning of life and how to honor God's commandments.

THE WORLD TODAY

Kids need a good role model to look up to. It seems as if things have really gotten out of hand and there are so many bad influences, especially in rap music.

I grew up listening to old school rappers like Run-DMC, Fatboys and Kurtis Blow. They were my favorite and I also loved Salt n Pepper.

The music was clean and many times there was a positive lesson to learn through the songs. I'm sure some of you remember MC Lyte, Poor Georgie these people are classics.

Now, I have Jesus in my life and He is wonderful to have in your life all the time and not just for the bad times. Sometimes, people don't realize that until it is too late. You can't make it if you don't have God. I had to find that out for myself. I got saved and I got my act together.

MY ANGEL

I had a close friend who was a teacher at East Meck. One day, I opened the door for her because she had a lot of books in her hands. I was just being nice and asked if I could help her with the door. She said, "Thank you young man for holding the door for me."

We became good friends and she did so many wonderful things for me and my mom.

Because of her, someone donated a brand new Macintosh computer to me.

It was a very good computer and I'm sure it wasn't easy for her to get it for me.

I'm still very thankful to her for all the things she did for us. I believe that she was my angel for that season of my life. I met her son, he is a good kid. I also met her husband and daughter. Her husband was a great person to me. She moved to Spain and I miss her because she was a good friend to me. God bless my friend and her family.

She was always full of surprises, for instance, the day she gave my mom and I some tickets to a Charlotte Hornets' game against the Chicago Bulls. It was exciting to see my number one hero, Michael Jordan, in person.

I am a big fan of M.J. and that meant a lot to me because now I have good memories about attending that game.

I have many friends in wheelchairs, some of them I went to school with and I haven't seen some of them in seven years. I pray that they all are doing fine.

My friend Ty is a cool brother; I've known him for 14 years now. We keep in touch with each other and his wife. We met when I attended PAL after school; it was a place where they held meetings for disable people. We discussed things that we didn't like or problems that constantly annoyed us.

PAL stands for Program for Accessible of Living. They helped us with our problems and it was a nice place for us to hang out.

I know a lot of people going through difficult stages in their lives because of their disabilities.

My advice to them is, "Hang in there, God is on your side and you **will** make it.

FAMILY

My Aunt Evelyn (Catfish) is a wonderful person in my life; she is also like a mom to me. She has done so many things for me and she treats me like a son. That is something special!

She bought me some wrestling tickets to the big main event. This was my first wrestling match smackdown. I was so happy that I was able to go because I love wrestling.

She is one of the greatest persons I've ever known and I'm proud to have her as my Aunt. Her ex-husband, Ronnie is also a kind person and he always made sure that he made me feel at home.

I continued to pray for him and God has really blessed him. I love my Aunt Evelyn so much. I also love my Aunt Sarah, she loves church and she is faithful to the ministry. Teresa is funny and she makes me laugh. Regina is my aunt on my father's side. I can truly say that my aunts on my father's side treat me good also.

Family is so important to me. You must understand that life can end in funny ways.

ANGELS

Riding the city bus can be a hassle sometimes. Whenever I get on the bus, people act as if the world belongs to them. They see a disable man riding the bus in a wheelchair and the first thing they do is stare. You will find some that will offer help while the others continue to stare.

I had a bad experience about four years ago as I rode my power chair on North Graham Street heading towards Wayne's Supermarket. Suddenly, my chair cut off and I lost power in 90 degree weather in July 1999. There was nobody there to help me. I continued to try to get help but nobody responded. It took approximately 1 hour before someone decided they would stop and help.

I asked a man to help me by calling my mother and he thought I was asking for money. Finally, a Caucasian man stopped and pulled his truck to the side of the road and asked if I needed help. I said, "Yes sir, I do."

I gave him instructions on what to do because my battery had been disconnected from the back of my chair. I thanked him for his help and said, "Have a good day."

After he'd driven away, I told myself that he was an Angel watching over me and with that in mind, I made it home safely. It's hard to find good people like this man who took a chance to stop and help me. I truly believe that if he had not stopped to help me, I would have died in that hot weather because I have lots of breathing problems. God watched over me. "Thank You."

I have a close friend who was also my nurse and she is a kind person that goes out of her way for me. I remember times when my power chair batteries would die and she would get in touch with the company and take me there to make sure everything was ok. Even though she had other appointments, it didn't seem to be a problem of her staying with me all day. If I were her boss, I would give her a raise because of the way she spent time with me and helped me. I never stopped thinking about her because she made my life easier and made a difference in my life.

There was another Nurse's Aide that was a good friend to me. Writing this book causes me to remember all of the good times. When she was finished helping me in the mornings, we would watch movies. She is a very sweet person and I could never say anything bad about her. She was a great friend to me and she gave me advice on how to talk to women.

She never complained about her job and she made sure she did her job right. I'm glad that I had the opportunity to know her.

I've met so many good people in my life. So many, I cannot name them all. I do remember my friend I met at the MDA Summer Camp every June when school was out for summer. Mom and her friend took me to Rock Hill, S.C. so I could give my mom some time to be alone. He was my counselor at camp and he was also a good brother to me. We would hang out and have good times together. He always kept in touch with me when camp was over.

MA PEARL

I lost my great-grandmother on November 26, 2002. She was 91 years old and full of fire. It was a fire that you couldn't put out. She enjoyed life and didn't take it for granted.

She was a wonderful person who graced the earth for a long time, full of knowledge and willing to share it with anyone who was willing to listen... She would do all of the cooking for the holidays because she loved to cook.

My great-grandmother would cook homemade food like homemade pies, fresh collards green etc. . .

She was a loving mother who lived a great life. If you needed help she would never turn you down. Her spirit will always remain in our family. I can feel her presence with us all the time. I miss her big smile that brightened her whole face when she smiled at you. She was truly a rare pearl in our lives. I know that you are in heaven taking over everything and making others happy. We miss you Ma Pearl.

MY GRANDPARENTS

My maternal grandparents, J.D. and Sarah Davis, had 13 children. There are 7 boys and 6 girls who are all still alive.

My grandma Sarah is a good Christian woman. My grandparents have been married for 53 years. That is a long time of loving, caring and being respectful. I'm sure that played a big role in them staying together so long.

They both are a big influence in my life. I remember when I used to walk to school and my grandmother would worry about me because my legs would get tired and I would fall. Even though she didn't like me walking by myself, she knew that I would still be fine.

Both my grandparents would be standing on the porch waiting for me when I came from school. It felt good to have them both in my life as I grew up.

My grandparents kept me because my mother had to work; they did a good job in helping to raise me. My paternal grandmother, Mom Petty, has been a great support in my life. She has a lot of faith in me and always believed that I would write a book.

I love Mom Petty because she is keeping in touch with me more and I'm always happy to hear from her. I believe she really cares for me and what takes place in my life. She always places her family first and she has my blessings for being a nice person and caring for others. Mom Petty is my hero, just like my mom.

I pray for my family because life can come and go, so we need to thank God for blessing us with good people in our lives.

MY ROLE MODELS

My Uncle Sammy is a good and smart man. He is devoted to church and a good father to his 2 children. He has a loving wife of 13 years of marriage.

Uncle Sammy is a hard worker and I admire him for the man he is today. He is a good role model for me and I respect him. I have an uncle whose voice sounds like the late great Barry White. He has been involved with music for as long as I can remember. He is married with two beautiful daughters.

My Aunt Von is a wonderful person and she loves to sing, especially during holiday gatherings. I think she sounds like Toni Braxton.

I finally got to know my Uncle James, not because of anything bad but I was so shy and his voice was very intimidating. I finally got over the shyness and started to talk more.

I have an Uncle J.D. named after my grandfather. I hadn't seen him since I was a little boy. He moved away from Charlotte and no one had seen or heard from him in many years. The family finally got to see him for the first time in 10 years. He explained that he had been living in Florida and he wasn't going to stay but just came to visit his family. We didn't care because it was just good to see him and know that he was ok. My uncle has been through a lot in his life but now he is saved and trying to better himself.

Grandma Sarah was happy to see her son after waiting so long to see him. The greatest gift for my grandmother was to know that he was doing fine.

I pray that he would return home for good someday and I asked God to continue to watch over him and keep him safe.

I encourage you to pray for someone in your family and help them get through the rough stages in their lives. I'm sure they will appreciate your help and prayers more than you know.

My Uncle Carlos and Torrence were like my big brothers growing up at my grandma's house. They would watch wrestling and eat chips with me. Torrence was in prison but he has been out for three years. I used to write him and let him know that I was praying for him and that, "Jesus loves you and He will guide you out of prison."

I care about both of my uncles and hope things will get better for both of them. They have made a lot of mistakes in their lives but they are human just like us. People make mistakes all the time; you have to give them a chance to make a change in their life before you start judging.

Just think, if God decided to judge everyone on earth, how many can honestly say they would make it? That's why I ask God to give my uncles, Torrence, Hasker and Carlos a chance to do the same.

My uncle Hasker has had his ups and downs in life but he can't help it. He is good at making everybody have fun and laugh and he loves to dance and have a good time. He is the uncle that Bernie Mac always talks about at family gatherings. I think that my uncle can turn his life around and better himself. He's a caring person and I believe God will change his life.

My uncle Dexter has devoted his life to church. He always offers to help out if needed. He is also a good role model and I can say that I 'm truly blessed to have such a great family. I love everyone in my family and I accept them in any condition that they happen to be in.

MY DREAMS

I have dreams of becoming a movie star. I grew up watching Eddie Murphy, Martin Lawrence, Richard Pryor, Denzel Washington and Halle Berry. They are my idols and I am a true fan.

They have blown the box offices away with the movies they've made. I love Halle Berry and I think she is a beautiful and talented woman. I have seen all of her movies and she deserved the Oscar.

I wanted to be like all of the names listed above when I was a child. I would love to be a screenwriter, maybe in the future.

I had a dream for a long time that I was a well known writer and I was the first disabled man to become a screenwriter or famous actor. I wanted to show people that disabled people also have a lot of talent.

I also dreamed that I was rich and I was able to help my family and my ex-girlfriend. I'm tired of not having enough money to support myself. I feel as if I have to depend on people to do everything for me. I know that they don't mind because they love me.

I miss going to work. I worked at Pic A Flick Video for two years and I enjoyed working for them. I worked for Pizza Hut for two years. I have had 7 jobs and 6 years working experience.

I love to work hard and show that I am capable of doing my very best like everyone else. I love earning my own money and not have people giving me money as if I were begging for a handout.

Social Security cut my disability check. I don't understand them, first they encouraged me to find a job and be independent when I got older.

Support Unemployed Training helped me to find easy jobs to work, God helped me also and He assured me that I would have a job. He told me that I had a lot of talent to become a screenwriter. "I'm doing what God said do."

I have a lot of time to work on my book because I'm not working. All I do is watch television and get bored of being in the house all the time.

Sometimes I feel like I'm going crazy and I know I need to get back out there and get my life back. I'll have to start over by meeting new people and gaining my confidence back. I had so much to offer my family when I was working. My book and writing other stories seem to keep me busy for the time being. I can't wait to get back out there on my own.

APPRECIATING GOOD TEACHERS

I have memories of Ms. Simmons who was my homeroom teacher. She was very nice and always welcomed me with a bright smile each time I came to homeroom. Once she bought me a big school bag and a few other items. She was kind to me and I will never forget the nice things that she did for me.

I am proud to say that I received good grades in school. There was an English teacher who was good to me and I learned a lot in her class. She bought me some clothes when I was sick in the hospital.

My old junior high teacher died a while back, she was a good teacher. Many of my friends were sad about her passing away. I remember how she helped us with our homework and was always there for us.

Mr. T. was another good teacher. He was there when you needed him. Once we went on a field trip to watch the Charlotte Hornets play on their court. I met NBA players such as Dell Curry, Mugsy Bogues, Larry Johnson and Alonzo Morning. My favorite players were Mugsy Bogues and Dell Curry. Most of the players had a positive attitude and were friendly but there were a few who had bad attitudes. I was very disappointed about them moving out of Charlotte because they were the first NBA team here and they put us on the map.

I think the new owner of the Bobcats is going to be a good NBA owner. He's positive and he will bring entertainment also. I sometimes feel players are overpaid and they don't play for the love of the game. When I was younger it was more fun to watch. I'm not talking about all players, I'm sure they know who they are.

SHOPPING FOR ME

Clothes are really expensive when you are my size. I can't afford to buy clothes because they are too expensive. A pair of pants would cost me $85 and the shirt would be $45. I feel as if some stores discriminate against big people because it's really hard to shop for things you like.

My mom has to shop in the Big and Tall Store to find my sizes. I hate to go through that and I feel sorry for others that have to do the same.

I have to concentrate on my health and stop eating junk food. Sometimes I even have a strong urge for sweets. God told me I have to be strong and take my life more seriously. He said, "Put all of your strength in your heart so you can get over your fear."

It is really hard to lose weight and we must put faith in *us* to do that. Always have faith and do not courage and don't be ashamed of who you are. I know that it is important to talk to God everyday and He gives me plenty assurance that He will always be there for me.

You're not alone. Don't allow anger to stay on your mind and it's not good to have all that pain inside of you. I had to get all of that stress off me and God blessed my soul so that I would not have to go through all of that.

I'm a true believer in God and I trust Him to guide me and show me the way to happiness for me and my family.

I want to be loved and protected by you God. I want my children to be in good health like you've done for others. Everyone should take time out of you busy schedule and pray to God.

INNER THOUGHTS

My thoughts have painted a future of how the world should be a better place for us. Love comes from the heart; people should be truthful and learn to love each other. Share your blessings with others and you will receive your blessings from God.

I have much respect and love for God and I live my life to the fullest without regrets about my disease or how I've had to live my life.

I wish that people could only be more patient with me and try harder to understand what I'm trying to say when I speak. Sometimes I stutter when I talk and people don't fully hear me out before I can clear my voice to finish my sentences. I will admit that I get stressed about it but I have learned to take my time when I talk.

I have friends who are unable to talk or move their arms or legs and they depend on their parents to feed them. We must be thankful that we can do those things for ourselves.

I remember when hurricane Hugo hit Charlotte and no one suspected it would come so close to land. God said be prepared for anything to come your way. Trees were down and people came together to help clean up the neighborhoods. There were a lot of power outages during the storm but God saw us through it and kept us safe.

We should always count our blessings.

- Make God first in your life.
- Do not give the devil any room in your life.
- Trust God and He will fight your battles.
- The battle is His not ours. It belongs to God.

Just when we think God has not answered our prayers, He does. Sometimes we get so busy until we don't realize that He has already answered our prayers.

MORALS

It is my opinion that men should consider taking their marriage vows more seriously. When you ask the woman you love to marry you, that is one step closer to God.

I realize that I am not married and I don't claim to be a professional in this area. It is my opinion that when a man chooses to get married, he should be committed to his wife only. He should respect, love and try to understand her feelings. I think you should take serious the vows that you make before God.

Be a good father, go to church with your wife, and you will receive a blessing just the way they did in the bible.

I don't mean to sound preachy but I'm just telling the truth about how I see our role should be here on earth.

My advice to the women is the same, be a good wife to your husband. Treat him the way you would want to be treated.

Men, if your pride has taken over, ask God to give you the right words to say in order to get your wife back. Tell her how you really feel and admit when you are wrong.

It's your loss if you lose the woman who should have been your soul mate.

It will be too late to run back for her because she's probably given you more than enough chances.

Pride kills; I'm trying to help you brothers to see the true value in relationships. When you try to be players, you will find that what goes around comes back around. It hurts worse when it comes back to you.

If you're not ready to commit, be a man and tell her or you will find out, "Once a scorn woman, always a scorn woman."

You are playing with fire when you use these words and don't mean it. I LOVE YOU. You are playing with emotions, trust and feelings. Just do what's right and your blessings will come. Be a father, husband or a faithful boyfriend and you will see in due time that it was well worth it.

MEN vs WOMEN

I love watching WNBA basketball, especially Lisa Leslie, she plays for Los Angeles Spark. She has a lot of talent, not to mention she's smart and a beautiful black woman. I think they deserve the same respect that men are given on the court. Times have changed for women in sports. I remember when there weren't many women sports. Now they play as many sports as men do.

I am glad to see women compete with men. I have nothing but the highest respect for them. I love Charlotte Sting and I feel people should really support them. I haven't had the opportunity to see them play live but I watch it on ESPN along with the Williams Sisters. Those girls are bad!

They are a good role model for any woman today because they have a lot of pride and they didn't let anyone stop them from playing the sport they love.

Men shouldn't feel threaten because a woman can do exactly what they can do. God said He is very tired of people hating one another and it's time to grow up and learn to get along with each other. Stop treating people different and respect one another. If you don't teach the children anything else, teach them that.

FRIENDS

I'm blessed to have friends like Tracy, Eric, Janet and Sharon. They were my co-workers at Pic A Flick Video. They helped me all the time when I worked there. Tracy is a kind and sweet person. She would help me when the store would get real busy. She attends UNC in Charlotte along with Chung.

I was privileged to have such good people around me and they respected me for who I was. Joseph was my manager and he was very helpful. I learned to use the computer within 3 days of working. He had to move to Colorado to help run his family business. He was a great friend and manager. They all were good to me and they helped me with my shyness around others.

I think about them all the time. I had to quit my job because of Social Security. I could not continue to work and receive my monthly checks.

My mom's best friends name is Rosebug. They have been close friends since I was a young child. She is a true friend to my mom and they always celebrate each others birthdays together. They shared a lot of memories over the years. She has brought so much joy to my mom. You can talk to her and her man friend about anything. I call him big daddy Curtis; he is cool and down to earth. He always take time to talk to me and watch movies with me. We have something in common, we both like to watch old school movies like 70's 80's and 90's movie classics.

I know one day he will be a good husband for Rosebug. God loves to see people in love. It's not all about money, looks, or sex. *It's about love.*

Many times we get trapped in relationships when we fall for someone and they were not who we thought they were.

You can't change people but you can pray that they better themselves and put forth effort to change. If they refuse to do so, I think it's time for you to move on with God on your side. Trust in God to make you a better person.

BLESSINGS

My cousin Crystal was married on June 7, 2003. Her husbands name is Jamel. He is going to make a good husband for her because they have waited on this day for a long time.

Crystal has been a strong positive person in my life. She has been like a big sister to me. I love the conversations we have when she comes around. She really knows how to make me smile.

The biggest gift I ever received was on Christmas, 2002. I met my two half brothers, Ryan is 15 and Clark is 13. They came to visit me for the first time. Their mother is sweet and kind. I met her mother also.

I enjoyed learning more about my brothers' future and what they planned to do in life. Ryan is planning to attend college and Clark is thinking about going to college also. They are smart young men. I am proud of them and hope to be a good role model for them.

If my brothers ever need any advice on life, I will always be there for them.

They are so blessed to be able to walk and take care of themselves. I was glad for the opportunity to meet both of them. We will spend time together when school is out. They are the best friends and brothers I longed for as I grew up. I pray for them that things will continue to go well for them and their mother.

They are so important in my life. I love to see people have something good and important in their lives.

God wants us to have love in our relationships and trust one another. We must be thankful for every blessing God has given us.

Tell God that you thank Him for saving your soul from the devil and giving you another chance in life. God wants you to be strong in your heart to receive all the blessings He has for you and to be better in your relationship with Him.

LIVING WITH MD

Have you ever looked at a Jerry Lewis Muscular Dystrophy Telethon and wondered what it was really all about? Many people relate to him as the man who is always collecting money for those children in wheelchairs. It's sad that the majority of people never watched it long enough to figure out what was really going on.

The telethon is usually a 21½-hour, star-studded variety show that has entertainment, informs and raises funds for the service and research programs of the Muscular Dystrophy Association.

The telethon is about Muscular Dystrophy. It is a disease in which muscles of the body get weaker and weaker and may slowly stop working.

Once the muscle fibers are damaged, people with muscular dystrophy begin to have problems with the way there body works which makes it hard to walk.

Between the ages of 2 and 6 years old, the muscles in their arms, legs, and pelvis begin to grow weaker. This is the state I'm in right now. I have trouble breathing and my bones ache all the time.

Even though I was born with this, I have morphed into this unique person that is more in touch with this life God has given me. I am blessed to still have strength to write this book and smile and tell people I am a child of God. Though you may look upon me as handicap, weird or unhappy, I'm still a child of God.

I am somebody special who cares about the well being of others. I've heard so many people say, "Jerry's heart is as big as the universe and he always has a smile no matter what kind of day he was having."

"I made it through pneumonia, surgery, my intestines burst, muscular dystrophy and hearing doctors say that I was not going to live. . .But, I made it!"

"I am a child of God. Many people take life for granted. I live to enjoy life and that's the greatest thing you could ever do for you! "I LOVE MY LIFE!"

Confederate Soldier's Prayer

I asked God for strength, that I might achieve,
I was made weak, that I might learn humbly to obey.

I asked God for health, that I might do greater things,
I was given infirmity, that I might do better things.

I asked for riches, that I might be happy,
I was given poverty, that I might be wise.

I asked for power, that I might have the praise of men,
I was given weakness, that I might feel the need of God.

I asked for all things, that I might enjoy life,
I was given life, that I might enjoy all things.

I got nothing that I asked for - but everything I had hoped for.

Almost despite myself, my unspoken prayers were answered.
I am among men, most richly blessed.

(This poem was found on the body of a valiant Southern soldier, 1861-1865)
~Known but to God

Words from the Author

I received a brand new power wheelchair and it was the best gift I could have asked for because it has made it easier for me to get around. I believe that God will continue to take care of the cost as I continue to pay my tithes.

I don't attend church, but I'm saved. I send my tithes to the church because I believe in God. I know this is why so many good things have happened for my mom and me.

I don't read the Bible all of the time, God gives me all the words to write and say. I listen to Rev. Claude Alexander, pastor of University Park Baptist Church, in Charlotte, N.C.

Some of my family are members of his church and I love listening to him. He is a good preacher and I learn a lot from him as I deliver his message to others.

I've seen many of my friends not being able to speak, dress themselves, write with their hands or even feed themselves. It is hard for them and it's not their fault. It's nobody's fault, it just happened to us.

One day you're able to walk and support yourself and out of nowhere, your life changes. MD can make a turn for the worse and you can lose all strength in your arms and legs. Your muscles get so weak and you lose all of your independence.

It's like your soul has been taken away and you have no strength, no feeling in your body and it is a nightmare just as many of my friends has experienced.

I have lived with MD all of my life and there is no known cure for it. Just because you take medication doesn't mean it will go away.

Sometimes my uncles think that if I would lift my weights I can be strong again, it doesn't work like that for me or for anyone that has MD. All it does is put more stress on the arms, legs and brain. It creates more pain and makes it easier to beak your bones.

People can live up to 15-20 years or get older without knowing about this disease, it can strike at any age. It is important that people should be grateful that they don't have this disease. I don't have the worst kind of this disease but my situation can decline.

Well, I'm still living so far and I know how to face dying when my time is up. I'm not thinking about dying and I do get tired of people looking at me crazy when I'm outside or out in the public.

I keep a good spirit and nobody can take that away from me, not even the devil. I told the devil once when I was young that I wasn't afraid of him. I can fight him back with the power of God and prayer. I don't ever try to follow in his footsteps. I follow my Father in heaven and I pulled through, all because I pray and give my tithes to the Lord is the reason I'm still here.

Thank you Lord, for all of my blessings.

ADVICE FROM THE AUTHOR

Sometimes people don't know much about love or how serious it can get. See, love is a serious matter, especially if you don't know what it really is. Beware! Many times we get stuck in relationships that are unhealthy for us and we're unable to see clearly and it turns out to be a nightmare.

I said this in an earlier chapter, "You can't change people. All you can do is pray for them."

It's left up to them to trust God so that He can make them a better person. You have to put your past behind you and not look back. Live your life to the fullest and don't spend time regretting what you cannot change.

I pray that you have learned through reading this book, what this disease can do to you at any time. I encourage you to seek more knowledge about Muscular Dystrophy and help save someone who is less fortunate.

The next time you see a Jerry Lewis Muscular Dystrophy Telethon, remember me, Jerry Petty. Pick up the phone and make a pledge from your heart and give some kid a chance. Even when you purchased this book, one dollar of your purchase is donated to MDA.

I pray that you enjoyed my book and not only learned about the disease but how to treat people who are less fortunate and have disabilities that make them different from you. Don't stare when you see us, just speak to us because we are human and we also have feelings.

Always remember that our hearts break just like yours. Our hearts also love and forgive. Don't take life for granted. Live each day to the fullest.

It's because He lives, I can face tomorrow

I know He Cares for Me

A SPECIAL NOTE FROM CRYSTAL

Jerry, you have opened my eyes to what it truly means to live and enjoy life. I am so thankful to you for this. Even though I'm not around as much as I should be but when I'm around you, it is well worth it.

It is because of you that I come around for Christmas. I love your prayers that are so sincere heartfelt. You enlighten me with each conversation that we have.

Many times when I feel that life is bad and I have nowhere to turn, I can't help but think of you and all that you have been through. It helps me to realize that I am not the only person in the world with problems and my problems are only as big as I make them.

Jerry, I've never heard you complain once about anything that has gone wrong in your life. You give me a sense of peace when I'm around you and you make me feel like I should be doing more in my life. I wish you could have attended our wedding. I know you would have had a blast. Even though you weren't there physically, you were there in spirit.

Your spiritual letters and grandma gift (cast iron) were the best gifts. I almost like ironing!

Your letters were confirmation to me that God heard my prayers. I cried when I read the very words I said to God in prayer. Jerry, all I can say is, "I LOVE YOU and you mean so much to me.

Your Angel
Crystal

What is Muscular Dystrophy

Taken from www.remedyfind.com

Muscular dystrophies (MDs) are a group of genetic diseases in which skeletal muscles which control movement progressively weaken and degenerate. These neuromuscular diseases are caused due to defects in the genes for a complex of muscle proteins.

There are many forms of Muscular Dystrophy. Some manifest at birth (congenital Muscular Dystrophy), and others in adolescence (Becker MD). The most common types are Duchenne, facioscapulohumeral, and myotonic MDs. These three types differ in terms of pattern of inheritance, age of onset, rate of progression, and areas of weakness.

- Duchenne Muscular Dystrophy mostly affects boys and is the result of mutations in the gene that regulates dystrophin - a protein involved in maintaining the integrity of muscle fiber. The onset is between 3-5 years and progresses rapidly. Most boys lose their ability to walk at 12, and by 20 have to use a respirator to breathe.
- Facioscapulohumeral Muscular Dystrophy appears in adolescence, causing progressive weakness in facial muscles and certain muscles in the arms and legs. It progresses slowly and induces disability which varies from mild to total.

- Myotonic Muscular Dystrophy may appear at birth (DM1), or have a later onset (DM2). Its symptoms are myotonia (prolonged muscle spasm) in the fingers and facial muscles; a floppy-footed, high-stepping gait; cataracts; cardiac abnormalities; and endocrine disturbances. Persons with myotonic MD have long faces and drooping eyelids; men have frontal baldness.

ORDER FORM

Enclosed is my check or money order made payable to: Chosen Word Publishing

To assure prompt and accurate delivery of your order, please take the time to print all information neatly.

Name____

Address______________________________________

City__________________________**State**__________

Zip______**Area Code & Phone (   )**_______________

Quantity ordered_______

Price of book: **$12.95**

Shipping and handling $__1.50

$14.45

Send Mail Orders to:

Chosen Word Publishing, Inc.

P.O. Box 481886
Charlotte, NC 28269
704.527.2177

Also available online at:
www.chosenwordpublishing.com

Jerry Petty will be donating one dollar to MDA for every book sold.

If you would like to make other contributions to MDA, the contact information is:

The Muscular Dystrophy Association
1-800-572-1717

MUSCULAR DYSTROPHY ASSOCIATION

Fighting neuromuscular diseases through worldwide research, a nationwide network of clinics offering comprehensive medical services, and far-reaching professional and public health education.